Potions

CLASS

SCIENCE EXPERIMENTS FOR THE MAGICALLY MINDED

MORTIMER

EDDIE ROBSON

THIS IS A MORTIMER CHILDREN'S BOOK

Published in 2020 by
Mortimer Children's Books Limited
An imprint of the Welbeck Publishing Group
20 Mortimer Street, London W1T 3JW

ISBN: 978-1-83935-069-6

Design: Samantha Richiardi
Art editor: Deborah Vickers
Editor: Jenni Lazell
Production: Nicola Davey
Photography: Simon Anning
Model: Evelyn Allan

Additional images: © Shutterstock
(glitter) Lightkite & G.Roman
(stickers) Kostenko Maxim

Printed in Dongguan, China
9 8 7 6 5 4 3 2 1

Let's make some magic!

Contents

Welcome, curious pupil …

Have you ever wanted to conjure up fantastic potions and bubbling brews? You may think these things can only be learned in secret schools—but this book can teach you magic in your own home!

In fact, you may have everything you need to do these spells in your home right now. With a little training, you can create magical effects from ordinary, everyday things—and gain powers your family and friends would never suspect!

And for those who want to dig deeper into these secrets, we'll also show you the science behind the magic, so you can learn why these strange and wonderful reactions occur . . .

Everything **YOU WILL NEED** for each spell is listed at the start of the step-by-step instructions.

Get an adult to help!

Look out for these stickers. They tell you when an adult's help is needed to use hot or sharp equipment, and will give you advice.

Science behind the Magic

DISCOVER

the science behind the spells in these boxes throughout the book.

Make a Magic Wand

Before entering the world of magic, you will need a magic wand. The best kind of wand is one you make yourself—the magical bond between user and wand will be much stronger!

Here's how to do it . . .

YOU WILL NEED

- Wooden chopstick (or a BBQ skewer for a longer wand)
- Glue gun
- Brown acrylic paint
- Paintbrush
- Thin copper wire

Get an adult to help!

1 Heat up the glue gun and use it to spread a layer of glue around the thick end of a chopstick. Don't worry if it looks a little rough!

2 When the glue is completely dry, paint your wand using acrylic paint.

3 Your wand is nearly finished! Now to add the finishing touches ... wrap thin copper wire around your wand for a cool effect.

Why not add stick on jewels, too?

Abracadabra!

Troll Snot Transformation

A useful ingredient in many potions, troll snot is a strange liquid that is sometimes solid—and turns back into a liquid in your hands!

YOU WILL NEED

- Cornstarch
- Food coloring
- Glitter
- Water
- Wide, shallow bowl or plate
- Measuring cup
- Spoon

1 In your bowl, make a mixture of two parts water to three or four parts cornstarch.

2 Add food coloring and glitter.

3 Use a spoon to mix them all together.

If you punch it, it will feel hard!

4 You should find that if you push your hand slowly into the mixture, it's easy to push through. But if you do it quickly, the mixture will seem stiff.

5 This mysterious material can be squeezed into a hard ball, but it will ooze over your fingers when you relax your hand.

NON-NEWTONIAN FLUIDS

The **starch** in the cornstarch mixes with the water to make a **non-Newtonian fluid**. The starch **molecules** move slowly. If you try to part them with your hand too quickly, they won't move out of the way—that's why it feels solid. If you go more slowly, they'll move aside, and the mixture will act like a liquid.

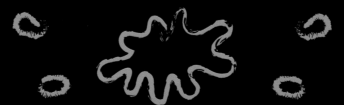

The Secret Script

Anyone who practices magic has secrets they want to keep away from prying eyes. With this spell, your words will disappear into the paper. Only a trusted wizard will be able to reveal the writing.

1 Squeeze or pour some lemon juice into a bowl.

2 Dip the cotton swab in the juice and write a secret message on the paper—as it dries it will disappear!

3 To read the message, hold it in front of a heat source, such as a very hot light bulb or an iron, and wait for it to warm up.

The message will magically appear!

Get an adult to help!

The secret is out!

Science behind the Magic

OXIDIZATION

Lemon juice doesn't show up on paper, but when it's heated it turns brown. This is called **oxidization**.

Unicorn Milk

Have you ever wondered how rainbows seem to follow unicorns wherever they go? With this spell you can create an amazing unicorn-enhanced rainbow of your very own!

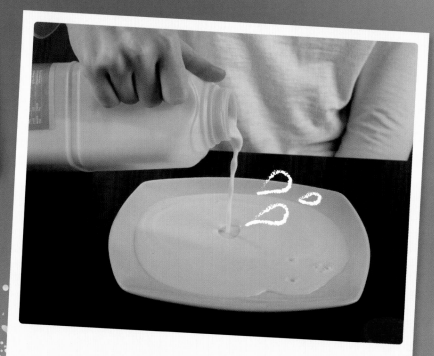

1 Pour a shallow layer of whole milk onto the plate.

2 Use a dropper or carefully drip 3–4 drops of food coloring onto the center of the milk.

3 Take your cotton swab and cover the end in dishwashing liquid.

4 Press the cotton swab on top of the food coloring in the milk.

Watch the colors race around!

MOLECULES

The crazy racing colors in the milk is all to do with the different **molecules** that make up these different liquids. Milk is made up of water and fat molecules. Dishwashing liquid molecules have two ends— one that attracts water molecules, and one that attracts fat molecules.

When the dishwashing liquid touches the milk, the dish soap molecules start grabbing onto the fat molecules while the other end sticks to the water molecules. The dish soap molecules race around, trying to gobble up the fat molecules—and they pull the food coloring along with them, which creates the patterns on the plate. Try using 2% milk or buttermilk to see the different reactions!

Popping Pixie Potion

This potion creates a delightful slime filled with tiny, invisible creatures that will POP their way into the real world. As you crunch and squish this supernatural substance, you'll be able to hear them escaping . . .

YOU WILL NEED

- White glue
- Foaming hand soap
- Shaving foam
- Baking soda
- Food coloring
- Glitter
- Contact lens solution (must contain borax)
- Measuring cup
- Bowl
- Spoon

1 Pour a cup of white glue into a bowl.

2 Pump a layer of foaming hand soap over the top of the glue, and add a layer of shaving foam.

3 Pour in the food coloring, scatter the glitter, and stir the potion with a spoon.

Choose your favorite color!

4 Add in a few drops of contact lens solution.

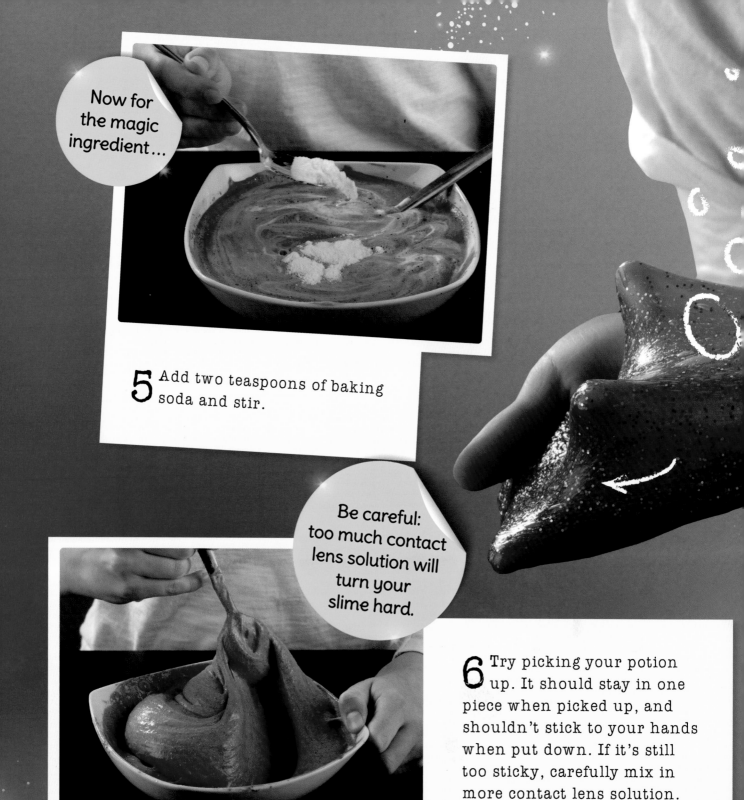

Now for the magic ingredient…

5 Add two teaspoons of baking soda and stir.

Be careful: too much contact lens solution will turn your slime hard.

6 Try picking your potion up. It should stay in one piece when picked up, and shouldn't stick to your hands when put down. If it's still too sticky, carefully mix in more contact lens solution.

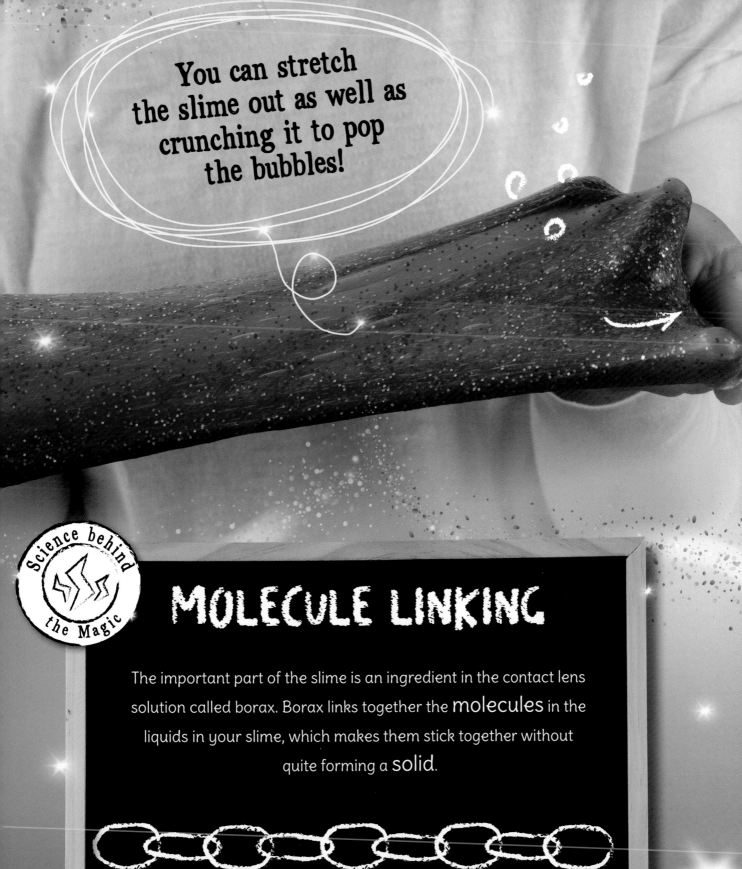

You can stretch the slime out as well as crunching it to pop the bubbles!

Science behind the Magic

MOLECULE LINKING

The important part of the slime is an ingredient in the contact lens solution called borax. Borax links together the **molecules** in the liquids in your slime, which makes them stick together without quite forming a **solid**.

Fountain of Fury

If you desire some spectacular, explosive magic to make ordinary mortals fear your power, this simple spell is for you. Take care—the effects of this magic are fierce and can be hard to control, so stand well back . . .

YOU WILL NEED

- Large bottle of fizzy drink (Diet Coke or Coke Zero works best)
- Mentos (half a packet)
- A tube roughly the same width as the bottleneck

1 Make sure your fizzy drinks bottle is at room temperature. Put the bottle outside on some flat ground, so it can stand without falling over.

Warning! This creates a lot of mess!

2 Put half a pack of Mentos into a tube so that they are easier to pour into the fizzy drinks bottle.

3 Open the fizzy drinks bottle. This works best when the bottle is freshly opened, so put the tube over the top very quickly and drop your Mentos in!

Stand back!

Science behind the Magic

CARBON DIOXIDE

The fizzy drink has **carbon dioxide** in it. When you open the bottle it starts to escape, but it doesn't all happen at once. When you drop the Mentos in, a huge number of carbon dioxide bubbles form very quickly on the surface of the Mentos and rush out through the bottleneck, taking the fizzy drink with them!

Weeping Werewolf

Can you stop a raging werewolf in its tracks before it attacks, and turn its anger into sadness? This spell enchants the werewolf to cry floods of colorful tears. But, remember, it can only be used on a full moon!

YOU WILL NEED

- Lemons
- Baking soda
- Dishwashing liquid
- Food coloring
- Wooden spoon
- Sharp knife
- Plate

Get an adult to help!

1 Ask an adult to slice a third of one lemon lengthways. Cut the other lemon in half, squeeze the juice into a bowl, and set it to one side.

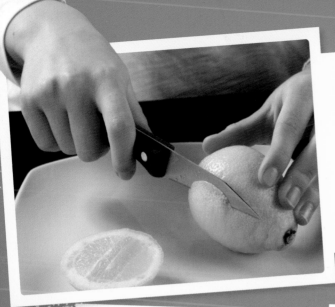

2 Cut a very thin slice on the opposite side of the lemon to make a flat surface for the lemon to rest on.

3 Poke the handle end of the wooden spoon into the first lemon and mush up the inside. Make sure the juice stays inside the lemon!

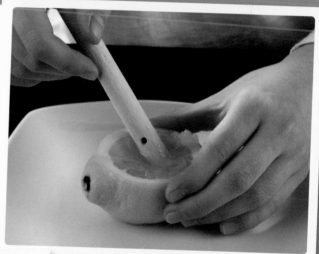

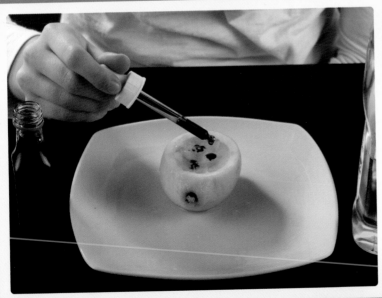

4 Put a few drops of food coloring and a squeeze of dishwashing liquid into the lemon.

5 Now drop a spoonful of baking soda into the lemon and watch it start fizzing. You can add the extra lemon juice to increase the fizz!

CHEMICAL REACTION

The **acid** in the lemon juice **reacts** with the baking soda to make **carbon dioxide** (like in carbonated drinks) and a salty liquid called sodium citrate. The bubbles rise and make the mixture fizz out of the lemon.

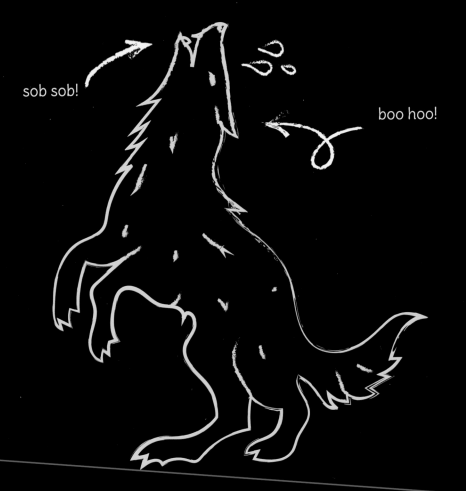

sob sob!

boo hoo!

Dragon Egg

With this spell, an ordinary chicken's egg can be transformed into something strange and colorful. What manner of creature might hatch from an egg like this? It must be something mystical . . .

YOU WILL NEED

- Raw egg
- White vinegar
- Clear jar (with an opening much wider than the egg itself)
- Food coloring

1 Carefully place an ordinary chicken egg inside a jar.

2 Cover the egg with vinegar and a few drops of food coloring. Leave for about three days.

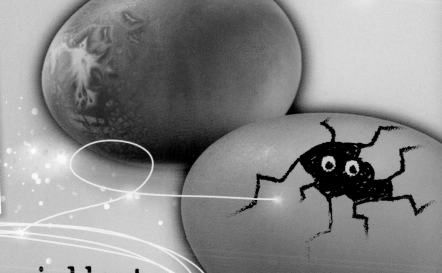

3 Pour out the vinegar and take out the egg.

Your egg should now be soft, bouncy—and colorful! But be careful, it can still break if you bounce it too hard!

What magical beast slumbers inside?

Science behind the Magic

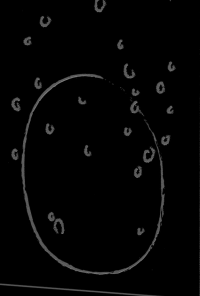

DISSOLVING

Did you see bubbles when you covered the egg with the vinegar? That's because the shell of the egg **reacts** with the acid in the vinegar to make **carbon dioxide**. The hard outer shell dissolves over time, leaving just the **membrane** underneath. Your egg will also have become larger as it absorbed the vinegar (and food coloring) through this membrane.

Dazzling Dream Lantern

A witch or wizard can see things ordinary people can only imagine. With a few simple materials you can construct this chamber to trap your dreams and make them visible. Watch as the colorful globs float all by themselves . . .

YOU WILL NEED

- Glass beaker or jar
- Vegetable oil
- Water
- Effervescent tablets (such as emergen-C)
- Food coloring
- Glitter

1 Fill one third of a beaker or jar with water, and then fill the rest with vegetable oil, leaving some room at the top.

See how the oil floats on top of the water.

2 Add several drops of food coloring.

3 Carefully drop a small pinch of glitter into the potion.

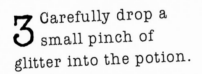

4 Drop an effervescent tablet into the potion.

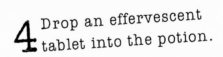

DENSITY

Water is denser (heavier) than oil, so the oil floats on top of the water—and the two liquids don't mix. Water **molecules** stick to other water molecules, and oil molecules stick to other oil molecules.

When the effervescent tablet is added, it **dissolves** in the water and releases little bubbles of carbon dioxide **gas** into it. This gas is lighter than the oil and, as it rises through the oil, it pulls some of the water with it. When the gas reaches the top of the oil, it escapes but leaves the water behind. The water droplets then fall back down through the oil, and the whole thing starts again.

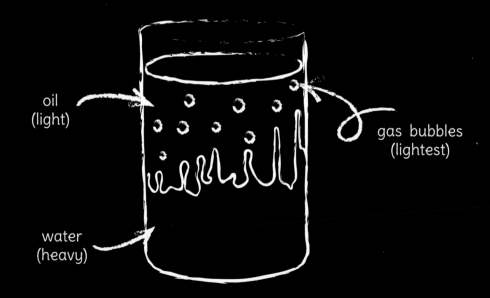

oil
(light)

gas bubbles
(lightest)

water
(heavy)

Shapeshifting Sand Sorcery

With this potion you can create a shape-shifting genie out of ordinary sand. It can transform itself into many different shapes—a useful spy indeed . . .

1 Pour about half a cup of white glue into a bowl.

2 Add a layer of shaving foam.

3 Scatter your glitter!

4 Add two teaspoons of baking soda and a squirt of contact lens solution. Mix everything together until you've created slime (see pages 18–21).

5 Fill another bowl with colored sand.

6 Tear off a small piece of your slime and work it into the bowl of sand, using your fingers to gradually tear apart the slime and mix the slime and sand together.

7 The enchantment is complete when the sand has a slightly crumbly texture, but can still be molded into different shapes.

STARCH

This sand slime is a bit like the stuff you buy in stores called "kinetic sand." The store-bought sand uses silicone oil to make it stick together, but ours uses the **starch** in the glue to do this job. The starch particles are attracted to each other. When you squish them together the particles cling together, becoming more **solid**.

Storm Sorcery

One of the most useful magical skills you can have is to control the weather at will. With this potion you can make it rain—indoors!

1 Fill about three-quarters of a jar with fresh water.

YOU WILL NEED

- Shaving foam
- Water
- Food coloring
- Jar
- Dropper

2 Spray a layer of shaving foam on top of the water.

3 Use a dropper to draw up some of the food coloring, and drip it onto the shaving foam. Watch the drops slowly fall through the foam and into the water.

Just like a raincloud!

Science behind the Magic

DENSITY

The food coloring is **denser** (heavier) than both the shaving foam and the water —so it falls slowly to the bottom when it has worked its way through the shaving foam. Just like rain falling from a cloud!

Swirling Slumber

This is the strongest sleep potion for young magic students. Just drop one of these concoctions into your bath and watch the water fizz with colors, aromas, and sleep magic.

Recipe makes six bath bombs.

YOU WILL NEED

- Baking soda
- Citric acid powder (available from a drug store)
- Cornstarch
- Epsom salts
- Water
- Vegetable or olive oil
- Food coloring
- Biodegradable glitter
- Essential oils
- Bowl
- Measuring spoons
- Whisk
- Muffin pan

1 Whisk together the following ingredients in a bowl:
12 tablespoons baking soda
6 tablespoons citric acid powder
9 tablespoons cornstarch
3 tablespoons epsom salts
1 pinch biodegradable glitter

2 In a second bowl, with a spoon mix:
15 drops of food coloring
4½ teaspoons of water
4½ teaspoons oil
½ teaspoon essential oil

Try lavender, lemon, or vanilla essential oils.

Stop any fizzing quickly!

3 Add small amounts of the liquid mixture to the powder and quickly whisk them together to stop any fizzing. Keep adding and whisking until the mixture is sticking together, but isn't too wet—like slightly damp sand.

4 Spread a small drop of vegetable or olive oil around each hole in the muffin pan—this will make it easier to get your bath bombs out when they're ready.

Run a bath, drop in your bomb, and watch it fizz!

5 Spoon a little of the bath bomb mix into each hole and press it down with the back of a spoon so the powder sticks together.

Leave the bombs to dry completely overnight.

CARBON DIOXIDE

The **starch** particles in the cornstarch make the mixture stick together when you press it into the muffin pan. When the baking soda hits the water it **reacts** to make **carbon dioxide** bubbles, and the rest of the bomb **dissolves** into the water, spreading the colors into the bath, and releasing the smell of the essential oils.

fizz!

Zzzz...

Fabulous
Phoenix Flight

One of the greatest skills a wizard can have is to summon mythical creatures. With this you can make a phoenix rise at your command!

Don't smudge the ink!

1 Blow up your balloon and, holding onto the end so it doesn't blow away, use a permanent marker pen to draw a picture of a phoenix on it. Once you've finished drawing you can let the air out of the balloon.

2 Half fill a bottle with vinegar.

3 Use a funnel to pour two teaspoons of baking soda into the balloon.

4 Fit your balloon over the top of the bottle and lift the balloon to tip the baking soda into the vinegar.

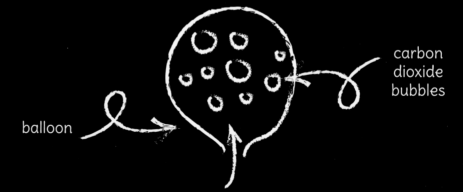

5 The vinegar will fizz, causing the balloon to inflate by itself.

Watch as your phoenix rises!

Science behind the Magic

CARBON DIOXIDE

The reaction between the **acid** in the vinegar and the **alkaline** baking soda creates a lot of **carbon dioxide**, which is a **gas**. The gas has nowhere to go but into the balloon, making it inflate.

carbon dioxide bubbles

balloon

What came first, the phoenix or the flame?

GLOSSARY

ACID AND ALKALI
All liquids are either acids, alkalis, or neutral (which means exactly between acid and alkali). Water is neutral. Acids taste sour, alkalis taste bitter.

CARBON DIOXIDE
A natural gas with no color or smell. We breathe in oxygen and breathe out carbon dioxide. It's also made by burning things, and when certain substances react with each other.

DISSOLVE
When a solid is placed in a liquid and breaks down until it becomes part of that liquid.

GAS
A substance which doesn't have a fixed shape, and doesn't stay in place in an open container. Air is a gas.

LIQUID
A substance with no fixed shape, but which can be carried in an open container. You can touch it, but it flows freely. Water is a liquid.

MEMBRANE
A thin layer of matter separating one thing from another.

MOLECULE
All matter is made up of molecules—they're so small you can't see them.

NON-NEWTONIAN FLUID
A type of liquid that can become more solid if you apply force to it.

OXIDIZATION
When a substance reacts with the air and changes.

REACTION
A change that happens when one substance comes into contact with another.

SOLID
A substance with a fixed shape. Wood is a solid.

STARCH
A white substance that can be found in many different plants, such as potatoes and corn.

STATE
The way something is at any given time. Most substances can be in the state of a solid, liquid, or gas.

SUBSTANCE
A piece of matter that's the same all the way through. A car isn't a substance, but the glass in the windows is.